Venice off the Beaten Track

N.Cimmino

Venice off the Beaten Track
N.Cimmino

To someone.

Venice on a foggy night. The author claims this is the best weather
in which to experience the magical atmosphere of the city.[1]
(Photo N.Cimmino 2016)

---

[1] Most of the author's friends disagree with this idea, take
it with a pinch of salt.

Preface

I have, for most of my adult life, wandered the alleys of Venice whenever I had a chance to. I did lose myself in contemplation of its beauty on countless occasions. Till I concluded, many years ago, that my appreciation for its beauty should be shared with others. So I started to dream of being, even if for just one day, the guide who is showing others around. I had a great occasion, soon after coming to that realization, to organize a long weekend in Venice for my friends and, to appear half-knowledgeable, took some notes in preparation of the event. At a later date, I have been coerced into publishing what I believe is just a little bit more than a short pamphlet.[2]

If you are looking for a detailed, historically accurate guide of Venice please go look elsewhere. I am terrible at names, dates and general history. If, instead, you wish you had a local to stroll with you through the alleys while learning something curious and unusual, that you wouldn't be told by

---

[2] This is the author's way to reject any claims of the product being unsuitable. You have been warned.

your average tourist guide, please go ahead and read.

If you have decided to tag along I suggest you get a map[3], peruse the guide to get an idea of where we are heading to, and then venture on the field to see for yourself.

A view from Accademia bridge.
(Photo N.Cimmino 2019)

---

[3] Hint: it's already in your pocket. No, I didn't sneak it in there, it's in your phone. It even comes with a fool-proof blue "you are here" dot that keeps stalking you.

Introduction

Venice looks like a fish! Whether you came in by boat, by rail or by road it should be immediately apparent to you that Venice, indeed, looks like one of these aquatic creatures. This, assuming, you were looking at a map when you were approaching the city.

So, what is Venice? Well, surprise surprise, it is a city! In Italy, northeast, even though I met people thinking it's in the south or west. Why should you visit it? You have been told it's full of tourists and stinks, haven't you? Well, it might be true if you pick the wrong period. Don't be sheepy, August is not the best season for any city visit, let alone Venice. Go to the beach in August: Venice Lido, a short boat ride from the city, and the whole Adriatic coast are waiting for you. When you are done bathing come back in winter or at least in autumn. If you are lucky you will visit on a foggy day. Nothing is more magic than the atmosphere created by the fog in the narrow, winding alleys of Venice. In case you are not so romantic to appreciate this kind of beauty, think at least it's going to be much cheaper in this season[4].

Who invented Venice you might wonder? Well, it's not been properly invented. Like most cities, it grew in time, a long time. Already in the 400s CE, populations from mainland fled to the little islands of the lagoon as barbarians invaded their land.

People living in the area were already familiar with the perils of seafaring having been, among other things, fishermen for a long time. They also had experience in building stilt houses so the natural choice, when the bad guys came forward burning and looting, was to move to the little islands of the lagoon and settle there. A move that protected them from the Barbarians, less acquainted with the element of water[5].

Historians have determined that a place nowadays famous with tourists, Rialto, was the first settlement from which the city developed. The "Rialto" name comes from "Rivus Altus" (Latin for "Deep River") which was the name of what later became the Grand Canal ("Canal Grande" in Italian)

---

[4] Caveats apply: even in winter, while generally the tourists' affluence is reduced, there can be special events that drive the prices up. Do your due research.

[5] Someone, namely my high school classmate, says the real reason they were safer in the lagoon is that they couldn't be seen thanks to the thick curtain of fog.

which, as you might appreciate, is pretty much the same expressed in different words.

You will notice there is no shortage of churches in Venice and we will encounter some along our route. Those who counted swear there are 139, I did not count so we will have to trust them.

Speaking of churches, according to the legend the first building in Venice was the St.James church ("S.Giacometto"), built in the Rialto area in 421 CE.

It's not only churches that abound in Venice, but saints are also all over the place. You might know Italy is a Catholic country and the saints are, by all means, the most common by-product of Catholicism. Even an atheist needs to muster the basics of saints in Venice as they are part of the address system! You will be directed to go straight to St.Fosca, turn left when you come to St.Formosa and then go straight until you reach St.Marco. The itinerary is purely fictional but that's how you could be directed if you asked for directions to a local. In truth, the places are squares or churches names but the saint name is often used alone to simplify the sentence. Anyhow, just to close on the issue of saints, the word saint is shortened with an "S." in Italian, always with a capital S. And, when mentioning more than one saint, the plural will be a double S, so you will see "SS. Giovanni e Paolo". Now you know!

Back to history. What was Venice like in 400 CE? Heck, I don't know, I was still in line waiting to be born and the guys at the time were lousy photographers. Anyhow, some other people better informed than me, say that the area was just a group of tiny islands, mostly muddy and covered in different sorts of vegetation. Not all the land we see now was above sea level. All Venice buildings have foundations that were made by driving wood logs, as long as twenty-five meters, into the muddy terrain until the more solid bottom was reached. Just to be clear we are not talking about four poles one at each corner of a building, we are talking about hundreds that make up the whole foundation.

Building on wood left rotting in muddy water? "That's a terrible idea!" I hear you crying. You might be excused for thinking so. However, a particularly densely muddy soil, aided by the high salinity of the water, provided an environment free from bacteria in which the wood, instead of going the way of your forgotten tuna sandwich, petrified and prevented the city from becoming a new Atlantis.

I don't believe this was sheer luck though given populations in the area had been building stilt houses already in prehistoric times. Even though they might have not known the chemistry behind it, I am quite sure they knew their wood was not going to rot.

Someone might have heard that Venice is sinking though, so you could conclude that these foundations are not so solid after all. Well, that is true. Venice has always been sinking. To overcome the problem of flooded ground floors, through the centuries, layers of pavement have been added to the sinking ground floors, in some cases up to 6 layers of thick stone! I suspect it was good to have high ceilings to start with, as without them the ground floors would have become suitable only for midgets. Keep your eyes open while we walk and you might notice some buildings with particularly low ground floors. Keep your eyes closed while we walk if you want a new set of teeth.

The sinking rate has increased during the last century. It seems this is due to the nearby industrial area, on the mainland, that drained groundwater reservoirs, allowing the bottom to slowly sink. Others say that the issue is chemicals in the water that are damaging the petrified wood foundations.

Enough talking! This is becoming a boring historical guide, let's move on to the first stop of our route: S.Lucia train station from where we can start some sightseeing.

Before we do though let me just clarify that, since at the moment of writing this guide maps on mobile phones have become ubiquitous, I will not be pedantic, as guides in the past used to be, with instructions on how to reach places. It will be very simple to follow along on your mobile phone map, just by the places name I will include describing the route to take.

S.Lucia train station

Normally stations would have the name of the city and, to be honest, this makes a lot of sense; you know, for those rare cases in which you look at a map and say: "I want to go to Rome, I will buy a ticket for Rome". Well, also Venice is no exception. The railway station is called "Venezia" but, even on your ticket, it will be fully spelt as "Venezia S.Lucia".

S.Lucia station main entrance.
(Photo N.Cimmino 2016)

This is mainly to distinguish it from the other "Venezia Mestre" station that is on the mainland.

Why on earth does a station have a saint's name? Let me tell you a story which will shed some light. When in the 1860s the railway was built the only good area for the station was occupied by a church, S.Lucia church to be precise. So it had to be demolished to make room for the new trains terminal. Given the high concentration of churches in Venice, I think this was no fate, but merely a probability matter. I assume whoever took on the project must have been scared to end up burning in hell and hoped, by naming the station after the saint, to save his soul. It could also be that the locals, being used to call the area "S. Lucia", just kept doing the same when the station was built.

It is a very common practice for Catholics to preserve every kind of saint's relics: bones, flesh, fingernails and teeth can be found in shrines in most churches. Poor S.Lucia was no exception and miscellaneous parts of her body were preserved in the church that was destroyed. The remnants were moved to the nearby (300 metres, 300 yards, 0.2 miles, 700 cubits, 164 fathoms) church of S.Geremia. We will come to that later, as soon as we get moving along our route. But first some more trivia about the railway station.

In 1860 a railway bridge was built that connected the mainland to the island and the first version of the station was built. This is relevant not only because it made Venice accessible with something else than a boat, but also because it changed the way people moved around the city. Up to that moment, the focal point of the city had been Rialto and people moved about by boats in the narrow canals and the Grand Canal. The area where the station stands now was, in fact, a secondary area on the outskirts of the city. Due to the general laziness of people, who refused to pack an inflatable boat to continue their journey once they arrived in Venice by train, more and more persons were walking from this area to the Rialto area through narrow alleys that had never seen a lot of pedestrians before.

I was not there but, if by the end of the 1800s a commission was set up to plan massive destruction of old buildings to open a wide road between the station and Rialto, they surely must have had their reasons. And that's how, by the beginning of the 1900s, the so-called "Strada Nuova" ("New Street") was born. It's been dug tearing down entire buildings and partially dismantling others. As a result, it is a rather wide pedestrian passage that goes all the way to Rialto. It does come with a peculiarity though: a bottleneck in "Calle del Pistor". We will see later why. Don't hold your breath, it's quite trivial and we have some walking to do before we get there, so you will need the oxygen.

Some more irrelevant trivia about the rail before we move on: the bridge connecting Venice to the mainland is roughly 3.9km long. Another historically relevant fact about the bridge is that I have walked it in 2012, on a hot summer day, and cycled it in 1994. Less importantly, from a historical relevance point of view of course, somewhere in the 1930s someone came up with the idea to build a road bridge along the railway. You would be excused to think that a road, ending on an island where the streets are so narrow you can barely walk, sounds like a crazy idea. This sentiment must have been commonly felt as they soon built a parking garage too. The garages are now three, and they are charging at the tune of what is, at the time of writing, thirty euros per day to park your car. So, in hindsight, it is not such a crazy idea.

The bridge was originally called "Littorio", a word that relates to the fascists' symbolism. For this reason, it has been renamed to "Ponte Della Libertà" ("Freedom Bridge") after WW2 when people became slightly upset at the previous regime.

One last bit of trivia that could actually come in handy: in case you have been forced into a date against your will you could set up an appointment at track 20 of Venezia S.Lucia station. This is the equivalent of setting an appointment for February 30th: despite the station having platforms up to 26, it lacks number 20 for reasons that are not known to the general public[6].

Let's get moving on towards the East till we pass "Chiesa Degli Scalzi", which is really a short form of "Chiesa Dei Carmelitani Scalzi". In case you haven't learned Italian yet, this literally means "Church of the Shoeless Friars". I think they were a bunch of guys that were not afraid to get HIV from infected syringes lying around in the parks. One of the statues on the front is missing, so look up and see for yourself. If you think a juicy and useless piece of history hides in the empty niche I am afraid you will be disappointed, I have no idea where it's gone. There are accounts of it being "tragically lost", but I could not find anything more. As they say: keep moving, nothing to see here.

---

[6] The term "general public" is used here loosely to indicate the three persons outside the station I enquired about platform 20.

To the west of the station is this bridge, which is the newest of the bridges over the Grand Canal. It is also one of the most controversial. While not included in this walk it is mentioned later in the text when talking about bridges.

(Photo N.Cimmino 2018)

Lista di Spagna

Passed the church the road narrows a bit. We are here in "Rio Terà Lista di Spagna". Let's start from the first part of the name. "Rio Terà" is a Venetian expression that indicates a narrow canal ("Rio") that has been filled up with dirt ("terà") to make it into a street. It's also one of the emblems of a recent struggle between Venice municipality and its citizens. I will not go too much into details here, as they would be quite meaningless for non-native speakers, the bottom line is that the municipality decided to translate alley names, that had always been in the local dialect, into Italian. In doing so, though, they often made crass errors revealing ignorance of the city's long history.

The row on the names, which is apparently still ongoing, has seen citizens armed with black paint "fixing" the new signs during the night in an attempt to restore the traditional names. You might be able to admire some of these "fixed" signs along the route, keep an eye for black paint marks on places names!

Since we are talking about this, street names in Venice are painted in black on white background directly on the walls of the houses. These white boxes are called "Ninsioetti" which in local dialect means "little bedsheets".

The white marble giving the name
to this particular stretch of road.
(Photo M. Fleischer 2015)

Coming to the second part of this place name "Lista di Spagna": this in Italian means "Spanish List". The name comes from some white marble stripes ("Liste") that were placed in the vicinity of embassies to mark the stretch where certain ambassador special benefits applied. Spanish embassy happened to be along this street and so the people referred to the place as "Lista di

Spagna". I know you are in a hurry to get walking but, if you bare with me for a while I would like to introduce you to the most common names you will find in Venice. If you absolutely want to get walking, skip the "toponymy" paragraph and move on but be warned, unless you read you will never know.

Venice off the Beaten Track

N.Cimmino

Toponymy

I would like to spend a few words on Venice toponymy and address system as both are pretty unique in the world and radically different from what you would find anywhere else in Italy.

A "Nisioletto", a distinctive element of Venice architecture.
Look out for these to see in practice the toponyms mentioned here.
(Photo M. Fleischer 2015)

First of all, while most cities have the equivalent of "road", "street", and "square" in the local language, these toponyms are not found in Venice.

There are a few rare exceptions which are due mainly to Napoleon paying a visit to the town. The first thing to remember is that Venice had no pedestrian traffic of any relevance for centuries. Buildings were always facing the water and people entered then from the waterside. Obviously, this happened after rowing a boat there as I believe swimming was not very popular. There happened to be some space between buildings just because when you put up your wall you didn't want to rest it against your neighbour wall.

These narrow spaces between buildings have been used to walk and ride horses since bridges over canals were built. These are usually called nowadays "Calle" from the Latin word "Callis" which means "path". There are over 3000 "Calle" in Venice each with a name usually of a nearby church, a profession or the surname of some famous person.

Names have historical origins and have not been assigned by someone sitting in an office, as is often the case in modern cities. For instance "Calle del Forner" (Baker Street quite literally, in case you are familiar with London) must have been named by people because a baker was somewhere there and, when they were giving each other directions, they were referring to the baker.

This brings up another issue: names are not unique in Venice. There might be several "Calle del Forner" for instance. This is irrelevant though as the addressing system doesn't rely on street names at all, they are just there for locals to give directions in the area.

I know, I know, you are hitching to know how the postal system works given street names are not relevant. That's why I'm going to tell you. Venice is divided into six districts, known as "Sestiere" (roughly meaning 1/6th). All the buildings of the area are numbered with a unique number. Numbers follow more or less a progressive order but, being this an area and not a single street, you might have a hard time sometimes to find the exact number you are looking for. Keep in mind there are a few thousand numbers in each area. So, your official address where mail is delivered will be something like "Cannaregio 123". Of course, everyone, except you, knows that numbers in the 100s are somewhere behind S.Fosca going towards S. Provolo (completely fictional, though the saints' names are real, which is, of course, the main point).

"Calle" is not the only street denomination in Venice. You can find "Salizada" a name deriving from the Italian name for flint. These were the first passages in Venice to be covered in flintstones (no, not "The Flintstones"). These were usually the most important passages and among the first to be covered in some sort of stone. Others, less important ones, were either left as dirt or covered in red bricks which were lined up in a slant pattern. There are very few examples left in Venice of this type of red bricks pavement. If you want to take a detour you can go to "Chiesa Della Madonna Dell'Orto", just North of here. Go ahead, I will wait here, it's not like I got anything else better to do.

You will also find "Sotoportego" (which translates to "under the porch"). This is usually just a narrow passage under a house porch. Don't be intimidated, it's still public thoroughfare[7], you might find some magnificent photo spots under these porches.

There are places called "Campo" and "Campiello", literary "Field" and "Small Field". These were large and not so large spaces between the houses that were used to keep animals and grow plants in a sort of little urban farm. They have also been later covered in stone and serve nowadays as squares. Some of the larger ones are used for markets, others have benches where people can sit and watch the world go by. It's most common to find a well, now disused, in the middle of a "Campo". If you see one look around it and notice some slabs of

---

[7] Hint: when you see someone sitting on the throne or taking a shower you have gone too far and through some door.

white marble, with holes in them. These served to fill, with rainwater, the reservoir under the well since there were no drinkable sources of water under Venice. This is also why the wells are not in use anymore.

The next one is "Corte" (more or less a "Court"): a space between houses, which usually has only one entrance and, at its best, will have another side leading to the canal. So most likely if you enter something called a "Corte" you will have to go back. But don't rush, have a look around first and snap some pictures, some of these can be very quiet and picturesque.

"Fondamenta" (meaning "Foundation") is another name you will find a lot. It indicates the exposed part of a building foundation which has been made into a waterfront passage.

"Fontego" is found in places that used to be goods warehouses. The name comes from Arabic "Funduq", a warehouse. There are two "Fontego" left in Venice: "Fontego Dei Turchi" e "Dei Teschi" (Turkish and German warehouse respectively). As someone might have guessed they owe their name to the fact they had been used by merchants from these countries to facilitate their commercial ventures in Venice.

Coming to the more common, in Italy, name "Piazza", which just means "Square", there is only one of them in Venice! That is Piazza S.Marco, which is along our route and you surely have heard about it already. We are not quite there yet, so you will need to be patient.

Next in our list is "Piscina", literally a "Pool". This name was assigned to a closed body of water between buildings. According to some sources it was used to preserve fish (to be clear, as fresh as in alive and swimming) before refrigerators were invented. Other sources quote them as being used for bathing. There are only a few left, as most have been built over, I presume due to the insalubrity of a closed body of water.

I have a few more. "Ramo", literary branch, is a small passage that sometimes connects two main roads, more often than not though it leads nowhere or into water. This is good to know, when roaming around without a map you can avoid, most, of the tracking back by avoiding entering anything called "Ramo".

Finally "Ruga", which I always found a bit gross as it means in modern Italian "Wrinkle", is a street that has shops on the sides. One might come to the conclusion that these shops were selling anti-wrinkle creams but, sadly, the truth is much more simple: the name came from the French "Rue" which, should you not be fluent in French, boringly enough just means road.

These are the most common names, in the end, they are all streets and squares, just they are not called like that. We might conclude that people in Venice are very particular about their place names, but we will not do that, just to avoid upsetting anyone.

Enough for the first 50 meters of the walk! Let's move on towards S.Geremia, Campo S.Geremia to be more precise which is, surprisingly, located in front of S.Geremia church.

Venice off the Beaten Track

N.Cimmino

S.Geremia

I don't know, and I am not inclined to find out who S.Geremia was. Enough to know that this is the church where the various body parts of S.Lucia were moved after the railway station was built. This place though has a much more important historical significance: this is where, sometimes in the early 2000s, the only car that ever wandered around Venice stopped. A group of, clearly drunk and bored, youngsters managed to drive from the road coming to the parking lots near the railway station over a pedestrian bridge to end their visit to Venice here, fortunately without injuring people on the street. It's also where hostel Alloggi Geremia is located, which is the first place I spent a night in Venice way more years ago than I care to remember.

There is more than just churches in Venice though, and in this "Campo" we find Palazzo Labia, which is the headquarters of the regional section of Italian national TV: RAI. I have been asked why a palace has a name that one would expect to find in an anatomy book (don't tell me you were not wondering!) so I went and found an explanation. Unfortunately, it has nothing to do with anatomy, nor with other juicy stories you might have concocted in your mind. The palace is named after a quite powerful Venetian family. Some might be wondering now why a powerful Venetian family had such an anatomical name. I have no story to report on the issue, but I do have a piece of trivia related to the family in general nonetheless.

One member of the family reportedly one night had a very sumptuous ball. To show how powerful and rich he was rather than giving silverware to his guests he had the servants to prepare the table with golden cutlery.

Palazzo Labia, in Campo S.Geremia.
(Photo M. Fleischer 2015)

Once they were done stuffing themselves with food he ceremoniously opened the window and threw out all the goldware into the canal that runs at the back of the palace. Those better informed reported though he had set a net in the canal and sent promptly the servants to recover the precious utensils. If you don't believe they managed to recover everything you might want to try and scuba dive in the canal. You will either find some gold or catch leptospirosis, but hey, they both would be free, so well worth a try!

A view of a street market from "Ponte Delle Guglie".
(Photo N.Cimmino 2018)

Ghetto

Moving on along the road, which is known by people as Strada Nuova, but is not (Strada Nuova being only one stretch of road later on in our walk), we come to "Ponte Delle Guglie" and turn left, after passing the bridge, onto "Fondamenta Cannaregio". Remember "Fondamenta" are the foundations of the houses and here we can see the exposed part of the foundation on which we walk. Here we enter the Venice Ghetto. There is a famous kosher restaurant, I have never been there but it is in my plans to give it a try.

So, about the Ghetto. It appears this was the first Ghetto in the world! It has been instituted in 1516. Surely not something to be proud of but an interesting piece of trivia for sure. The name Ghetto itself comes from the Venetian dialect. Though historians and linguists have been debating between two possible origins, both theories had words from the Venetian dialect at their roots. The first possibility is that it would come from "Getto", which is a "jet". Mind you, not in the aeroplane type sense, remember we are talking about 1516 here! The ghetto was created in an area where a dismissed foundry stood and, as it goes, foundries have jets of molten metal. Sounds a bit weak if you ask me. At any rate, the second possible origin is "Borghetto", something sounding like a "cute little village" to an Italian speaker.

A plaque paying tribute to the Jews
who fell during the First World War.
(Photo N.Cimmino 2018)

This is not official but my theory is that it truly comes from "Borghetto" but, since it must have pissed off a lot of people to define a ghetto a "cute little village", someone came with the "jet" theory. Also, my very personal belief is that some amount of wine must have been involved in naming the two parts of the ghetto (new and old) which are swapped: "old" is the name given to the newest part! There is some sort of rationale behind this in that the old ghetto was built on the older foundry, or so I have been told, one evening, after I had some wine....wait...or was it the other way around?

Back to the ghetto. Jews were forced to live exclusively in this area and, in many historical periods, were not allowed to wander outside at night while, generally, during the day they were allowed in town. According to statistics, there are about five hundred jews nowadays in Venice.

Those who know me personally also know what a film buff I am, so I cannot refrain from mentioning a famous 2004 Michael Radford film: The Merchant of Venice. Starring the great Al Pacino, the film was such a great success that Shakespeare decided to write a play about it. The film was partially shot in Venice and depicted the Venice Ghetto, so that's why it's relevant here.

Let's leave the Ghetto through Calle Farnese and get back to Strada Nuova through Rio Tera' Farsetti.

A view of the ghetto.
(Photo N.Cimmino 2016)

Strada Nuova

This stretch of road is the one improperly named "Strada Nuova" (new street), as people refer generally to the whole main road between the railway station and Rialto as "Strada Nuova". It's called "new" as it was dug between buildings, by destroying them, in the late 1800s to accommodate the increased pedestrian traffic brought to town by the railway. As we mentioned in the beginning, the project to tear down some buildings and downsize others to make room for the new street went on flawlessly with the results we can see today except in this spot. Here in "Calle del Pistor" we enter "Rio Tera' Della Maddalena" which is ridiculously narrow when compared with the rest of Strada Nuova. We would like to imagine there were hydrogeological reasons that prevented the road to pass here or that, perhaps, a famous and important church was on the way. Well, you will be surprised to learn it was something far more important that was standing on the way: the house of the engineer that planned the whole operation!

While historically irrelevant, there is a small shop on this street on the right. This is a great spot for tourists to grab a bite or a bottle of water at a much more reasonable price than bars and restaurants. I have inserted this paragraph only hoping to get a discount from them, but something tells all I will get is an extra charge at the bar nearby.

You can get one of these sugar bombs in most bars. The slice on the left is from a cake made with pinenuts; the other one is a shortcake with apricot jam.

(Photo N.Cimmino 2018)

The toilet sign

Let's keep walking on "Rio Della Maddalena" till we come to a bridge. On the left is a place called "Vecia Carbonera" which means roughly "Old Charcoal Storage". This is a great spot to taste some Venetian "Cicheti": little bites usually washed down with an aperitif. After the bridge, we come to S.Fosca. I am not making this up, I told you directions would have been from a saint to another! We turn left into Campo S.Fosca, cross the bridge and we will be greeted on our left by one of the most beautiful pieces of art this city has to offer: a toilet signpost in which the male is climbing a wall to peek over the female on the other side of the icon. This sign, other than being hilarious, is synonymous with food for me. Pretty much the only reason I have walked down this alley is to get to one of my favourite restaurants in Venice: "Paradiso Perduto", in "Fondamenta Della Misericordia", a few steps from here. They serve great fish with a home kitchen ambience. If you ask me this place is a must if you stay in Venice.

Also, because this is the land of saints, let's not forget that just by the toilet sign is the entrance of a place called "Il Santo Bevitore" (the drinking saint), another good place for a glass of wine or an aperitif.

An unmissable landmark.

(Photo N.Cimmino 2018)

Ponte Chiodo

Enough with food and wine! Let's not turn left at "Fondamenta Della Misericordia", which would force us to sit at "Paradiso Perduto" and eat. Let's turn right instead and walk all the way to the end till we come finally to Ponte Chiodo. Translated this means "Nail Bridge". When I started researching its history I was hoping this would yield some interesting story about nails (the metal ones or toenails, anything as long as I could get an interesting tale here) but, boringly enough, it seems this is just someone's surname.

The bridge, nonetheless, is very remarkable even though it might just look like an old, insignificant bridge at first. This is the only bridge in Venice that kept the aspect all bridges in Venice had until the end of the 1700s. One particular detail is that it doesn't have any side protection walls. Obviously, our ancestors were much smarter than us and could walk on a bridge without falling out. Those better thinking say the truth is back then it didn't matter much if someone drowned as it was not customary to sue the municipality for such trivial things.

This seems like a good spot to talk about bridges! Some trivia: there are 417 bridges in Venice of which 72 are private. Guess what? Ponte Chiodo is one of them, I mean of the private bridges. Of all these bridges 300 are built with bricks, 60 with iron, and 47 are wooden. There used to be just 3 bridges crossing the Grand Canal. Unfortunately, since 11 September 2008, we got the fourth one. It is an ugly bridge, not only in my opinion but according to many pissed off residents. The structure is made of bricks and glass. The glass gets slippery in rainy weather and many fell on their arse as a result. Not only, but the architect was also so nice to include, along with a series of regularly spaced steps, a couple of sudden longer ones: a guarantee to fall your face first. The bridge was so hated by people that it was opened at night without even an opening ceremony. It can be found just west of the railway station if you care to go and have a look.

Speaking of steps: bridges in Venice didn't have any until the late 1500s as, back then, it was common to ride horses along the narrow streets and the steps would have been dangerous for the animals. In light of the story above, quite a testament to how animal welfare was far more important than human safety is nowadays.

Let's move back to Strada Nuova and follow it to SS.Apostoli where we shall turn left facing North, for the orienteering inclined.

Let's keep walking and turn right into Rio Tera' Barba Frutariol. This means "The greengrocer called Beard", please don't ask, I don't know! Probably a greengrocer with that nickname had set up shop there.

Ponte Chiodo.
(Photo N.Cimmino 2018)

Calle Varisco

This will lead us finally to Calle Varisco. This is a very peculiar one as it is the narrowest in Venice, measuring just 52cm in width! As far as I know, it is also the narrowest alley in Europe. We can walk it to the end for the sake of it. Be warned: just ends in the water though so be ready to walk back.

Assuming you haven't got stuck in the narrow "Calle", let's trackback South towards "Calle Larga Giacinto Gallina" which, as the name implies, is a wide "Calle" ("Larga" meaning wide). This will bring us to SS. Giovanni e Paolo hospital. As we discussed in the toponymy section plural saints call for a double S.

A colourful flowers' shop in a quiet alley. These spots make it
worth to stray off the beaten track and wander around.

(Photo N.Cimmino 2020)

SS.Giovanni e Paolo

I am quite confident that, by now, nobody has been run over by a bus, so we will not make use of the services provided by this venerable institution. It is nonetheless a remarkable looking hospital which, at first, most would mistake as a church. It was built back in the 1300s and has been, for centuries, one of the largest hospitals in Venice. Used to cure the wounded during various wars it also served, at times, as a refuge for pilgrims en-route to the Holy Land to keep them separated from locals and avoid spreading diseases. Then, sometimes in the 1800s, a short french guy came along and through a decree decided it was a waste to have so many hospitals in Venice. There was a large hospital, named the "Incurabili" (which means "Incurables"), as it had been originally built on an island to host people with the plague. According to this french guy, to whom we will assign the fictitious name of Napoleon, everyone had to be transferred there and SS. Giovanni e Paolo hospital was left unused and abandoned. Of course, you can imagine the surprise of the guy admitted for a suspected fracture of the pinkie when he was told he had to be relocated to the "Incurables Hospital".

Some parts of the hospital are freely accessible by the general public and, in fact, some host some form of free expositions, so feel free to peek inside.

The area in front of the hospital's main entrance is named "Barbaria Delle Tole" which, even for someone speaking Italian might not ring a bell. It does though if you speak Venetian dialect, which I happen to. The name means "Planks' Barbershop" which might sound a bit strange to someone. Well, back in the day, even planks used to visit barbershops: story end. Since I see you are still a bit perplexed I will offer a more credible explanation: this whole area was, aside for the hospital, not built up and, being close to the open lagoon, was used as a storage place for building materials brought in by sea. In particular in this area wood planks were piled up and, as they came in with rough surfaces, they had to be shaved clean before being of any use as a flooring material. Not knowing better, or having had a couple of glasses of wine too much, someone started to call this place the "planks' barbershop" and the name stuck till the present day.

Another interesting feature of this place is a statue of Colleoni riding a horse. Colleoni was some kind of warlord who guided many mercenaries expeditions in the 1400s. What is more interesting though is that this statue, dated 1488 by

Verrocchio, is the first equestrian statue that stood on only three feet, to depict the horse as moving. This was, at that time, a big deal and many attempted such a feat, however, they couldn't get a stable structure. Some cheated by placing improbable objects under the raised foot to achieve a four-point structure. An example of this is a very similar statue of Gattamelata in Padova which has a globe under the horse raised foot to keep the structure stable.

And it is no coincidence that I mentioned the statue in Padova. There is an important piece of legend to be disproved here. Many believe that this statue faces westward and the one in Padova eastward at such an angle that they look at each other straight in the eyes, supposedly in a challenging way. This is a very nice story and also easy to believe as, in the past, there has been some rivalry between the cities. However I wanted to verify the claim for myself so, one day, I set off and did my measurements. Standing with a compass under this statue we can see it faces towards 290 degrees North. The one in Padova turned out to have a bearing close to 350 degrees North.

Colleoni riding his horse, fearless stares in the eyes of his
arch-enemy in Padova. Or does he?
(Photo N.Cimmino 2016)

So, eventually, the one in Venice could be looking
at the arse of the one in Padova. However, given
Venice is slightly north of Padova it is not even
looking that way at all. See? You need to do your
investigation and not believe anything you are told.
If you go by that principle, you should already have
your compass at hand and have cross-checked I
haven't made this up.

Finally, in this square, we can find one of the most renowned bakeries in town: "Rosa Salva". It's a rather old institution that bakes some of the best pastry you are going to find in Venice. Depending on the period of the year you will find different kinds of pastry and also ice cream in summer.

If you happen to be around in October, the month of the dead, one type of pastry to look for is "Ossi Dei Morti" which translates to "dead people bones". They are particularly hard biscuits made of almonds and eggs. This is a good place to try a few, perhaps with a coffee or a cappuccino. If you haven't followed my advice and came here during summer, fine, have some ice cream, it's equally good.

After stuffing ourselves in cookies and coffee let's head south in Calle Tetta and right till we come to Ponte Tetta. This "Calle" and bridge have a name that sounds like "breast" in Italian but has nothing to do with it, it's just a surname, sorry. You will need to wait later in the walk to satisfy your lust when we will come to "Ponte Delle Tette" which, indeed, is related to female tits. I will not spoil the surprise for now and let you fantasise on the name. We are here for a much higher cultural reason: we are here for a bookshop.

If your relatives brought you here for a minor ailment would
you think they lied to you and your time is actually up?.

(Photo N.Cimmino 2016)

Libreria Acqua Alta

The name translates to "High tide bookshop" and it couldn't be more appropriate. This bookshop is located on a ground floor that regularly gets flooded when the tide is high. If you visit in the right season, at the right time, and you have some appropriate boots you might have the pleasure of book shopping with your feet in the water.

Alternatively, you could try the millennia-old trick of walking on the water but, honestly, the last one that managed that successfully is long dead and nobody reproduced the feat successfully afterwards.

This place has proclaimed itself the most beautiful bookshop in the world, as an inscription in black marker over corrugated cardboard testifies at the entrance. A couple of cute cats roam the place and sleep on the books. Inside you will find thousands of books, some older some newer, in several languages and in different conditions. They are kept away from the tidal waters in high shelves but, more originally, also in a gondola and in a couple of old-style bathtubs as well. At the back, you can climb up a staircase made of books and admire the canal over the back wall from a high vantage point.

Assuming you haven't loaded yourself with heavy books it's time for a quite long walk to the next point of interest. Let's follow this route back to "Ponte Tetta", "Calle Dela Madoneta", "Calle S.Lorenzo", "F.ta S.Lorenzo", "Calle Lion", "Fondamenta Furlani" to finally reach "Chiesa di S.Antonin".

There is no denying the books in this bookshop are placed on display in rather unusual ways.
(Photo N.Cimmino 2018)

Chiesa di S.Antonin

Brothers and sisters, we have gathered here today, in front of this holy place to thank the Lord for His great mercy, to repent of our sins and see the holy light....sorry got carried away! There is another, arguably far more important, reason for which we came to this otherwise not so special church: this is the place where one of the many incredible tales one can tell about Venice came to its grand finale but, before we get to that, let me tell you the story from the beginning.

It was the spring of 1819 and the Carnival had just finished. At that time it was common during the Carnival to have on display around the city, among other things, exotic animals. In this particular year among other animals was an elephant, its origin or name is unknown to us. After having been on display among noisy and festive passersby you can imagine it was rather nervous while it was being loaded on a boat in Riva Schiavoni, a few hundred meters south of this place. So the animal eventually decided to break loose and started to roam the narrow streets. Without success, the owner attempted to lead it back to the boat waving some food on a stick. As the animal started to get angrier and angrier it scared people on the street so police were called to the scene. They attempted, in vain, to shoot him with shotguns, the bullets merely denting the animal tick skin. All they could achieve was to get the animal even more scared and out of control. At some point, the unimaginable happened. The elephant broke through a church door, this very church we are standing in front of, and started to destroy everything inside till it had a bad idea to step over one of those tombstones so common in churches. The stone eventually collapsed under the weight of the animal that got trapped into the tomb. At this stage the army intervened shooting the poor animal with a cannon of some sort, to be honest, I couldn't find out what it was exactly but something larger than a pistol. The carcass was supposed to be buried on an island at first but it has been claimed eventually by some scientists and the skeleton preserved. It can be found nowadays in a museum in Padova, unfortunately, one of the many Italian museums that are not open to the general public but can only be visited by researchers or school groups by appointment.

Let's walk now through what, most likely, has been the route followed by the elephant and move south to Fondamenta Schiavoni where the story

began, we will then follow west towards S.Marco
Square.

Piazza S.Marco on a quiet, winter night.
(Photo N.Cimmino 2016)

Venice off the Beaten Track
N.Cimmino

Piazza S.Marco

For many tourists, this is the central point and main attraction in Venice. To be honest, while I like the place, I much prefer the winding narrow alleys and the quiet courts away from the crowds. Nonetheless, there are things to be told about this place, so I should get started. Since we came from Fondamenta Schiavoni the first place to stop is just on the side of the main church, by the bell tower.

The baker

First, if we look at the church terrace we will see a side entrance which has two red lamps at its top. During the night these lamps would be lit up. The lamps are not just any lamps: they are actually 30W incandescent bulbs that are replacing what used to be before electricity came about, oil lamps. Now, you will be thinking, who would go to all the trouble of installing two 30W light bulbs and take care to light them up every night? That was exactly what I was wondering, so I set on a quest to find out. It turns out that we need to go back as far as 1507, on a foggy morning when a baker was leaving home early to go to work. Pissed off for the early time, and probably sleep-deprived, he must have not noticed a guy lying dead on the street until he tripped over him. Even more upset, as his trousers were now stained in blood, he went to look for some policeman. Some say to report the crime others (namely me) say to sue and seek reimbursement for his now ruined trousers. It obviously was not his lucky day: once he found a policeman and the situation was investigated he was taken into custody as a suspect! You would imagine after so much adverse luck things could only turn better for the poor baker but, as the story goes, actually that was not the case. It turns out the deceased was a nobleman and the baker being, well, a baker, he was sentenced to death for the murder with no hope to appeal. He was eventually put to death here, in Piazza S.Marco as all the other criminals of the time. But luck couldn't always be against the poor backer. Shortly after his death, things started to turn bright for him (speak of luck!). Another nobleman, related to the murdered one, caught a rare and deadly disease. Being the good Catholic he was, he thought it would be sensible to confess his sins before dying. Many were awful acts which we shall not mention here as not to get censored, but, among the mild sins he committed, one is of particular interest to our story: he did murder the nobleman found by the baker and, but this is of little importance, he didn't mention the detail when heard in court. This caused the baker to be sentenced to death. The guy eventually died of the disease and, since mobile phones had not been invented yet, he never phoned home to inform relatives whether he was burning in hell or resting on a fluffy cloud in heaven. So that is something we will never know. The ruler of Venice, called Doge, was concerned about the mistake and issued a warning to the judges to be more careful with their decisions. Apparently after this event judges, before making any decision, started to repeat a sentence, like a mantra, that sounded like: "Remember, remember, the poor baker". For reasons that are quite obscure to me the Doge also decided to put the before mentioned two lamps to remember the baker, of course, they were oil lamps at the time. The fact is, there is no mention at all in the official registers of this incident so many assume this is just a legend, or it could simply have disappeared from the books to save someone's arse. Bottom line: we don't know why the lamps are there! Or at least I don't.

The bell tower

In front of the main church stands a belltower. You can climb up to the top deck, on a lift, and enjoy a magnificent view of the city. You might also want to synchronize your visit with the start of mass so you can listen to the bells from a few meters distance which is quite an experience. The belltower has also been the setting of a few stories I would like to share with you. The first one takes place in the early months of 1902 when some works were carried out to, supposedly, fix some damage to the structure. In the following months, the cracks on the walls of the belltower started to worsen and eventually the all thing collapsed into a pile of debris in July of the same year. Nobody was injured nor died so, in fact, this story is not that interesting for some who are more into that kind of gruesome drama. The belltower you see now has been rebuilt after the incident and looks exactly like the collapsed one. It took eventually 10 years to rebuild it. You can now proceed upstairs if you still feel like it, it stood there for over one century so probably it will not come down in the next half an hour.

Let's fast forward to a foggy late night of 1997. The last boat from Piazzale Roma is about to depart, the captain can't wait to get back home and is probably quite tired. You can imagine the surprise when he sees a tank, albeit a small one, lining up to board the ferry. A small group of armed guys prevents the other cars from boarding the ferry while another guy walks to the control deck and kindly, or maybe not so kindly, asks the captain to sail to Piazza S.Marco. The captain attempts to convince the guys to give up, but they have their plan and they want to carry it out. They eventually reach piazza S.Marco where the hijackers use some planks to get the tank out of the boat. They then proceed to break into the belltower and lock themselves in at the top. They also install a radio transmitter on the terrace and broadcast messages that reveal their intentions. They are Veneto separatists and want to claim the independence of the Veneto region. Meanwhile, a French tourist, who was on the ferry, goes back to his hotel and tells the receptionist about the tank on the ferry. The receptionist dismisses the guy assuming he was drunk, and doing so he misses the opportunity to witness history. Soon police surrounded the tower but the situation was at a stand-still until about 8 AM when a special squad intervened and arrested all the guys.

Lions and churches

There are also a few lions, stoned ones...no no, I mean, stone ones as in not alive ones, in the square. The lion was the symbol of Venice republic. These lions are particularly educated as they have been reading books for centuries. On the book is the inscription "Pax Tibi Marce Evangelista Meus" (meaning "peace to you my evangelist Mark"). There were many lion statues in Venice before the aforementioned french guy came visiting in 1797. During a war period, they were represented holding a sword. As of today, 13 lions can be seen in "Piazza S.Marco", you can have a look and see if you can count them all.

There used to be as many as five churches around "Piazza S.Marco". "S.Marco" itself, "S. Basso", "S. Geminiano" which has been destroyed, "Ascensione" also destroyed, and "San Moisè" which still stands. So, doing the maths, three survived.

Health and Plague

Let's head back south towards the water, in Riva Schiavoni. If we look towards the south we will see, on the other side of the Grand Canal exit into the lagoon, a large white church. This is called "Madonna Della Salute " (which roughly translates to "Health Virgin Mary") and is the second church we are going to talk about in this story. The first is farther and, if the weather is suitable for this visit (foggy), you might not see it at all. That's Chiesa del Redentore (Redeemer church). These two churches are both linked to a history of disease, death and traditions that survive to the current day.

We need to go back to 1575 when a plague outbreak hit the city. In two years over 46000 people died. Nothing could help, there were no medicines, no precaution or sanitary restrictions that seemed to help the situation. Until, one day, someone had a bright idea: let's build a church (another) and pray to God that the pestilence will be over. So they did, unsurprisingly, the plague receded instantly. It was 13th July 1577, the 2nd Saturday of July that year so, logically (don't ask me what kind of logic), the city ruler decided that on the 3rd Saturday of July every year they would have had a celebration. He decided there would be a procession to give thanks to the almighty for being so kind to have stopped killing people for no apparent reason. And so they did, and still do, every year in what is known in Italian as "Festa del Redentore" or, to the locals, simply as "Redentore". The 3rd Saturday of July people gather in the alleys, bring tables and foldable chairs along with home-made food and loads of wine to spend the evening and night having a picnic with friends and relatives. Others spend the night on boats along the canals and in front of S.Marco square having their food on the boat and usually playing loud music. A floating bridge is built to connect the Giudecca island and allow people to go in procession to the church with no need to swim. A very long and magnificent fireworks display is held at midnight and the best place to see it is Piazza S.Marco. As fireworks are shot from the water basin in front of it, this is a pretty good vantage point. Be prepared to get there hours ahead though if you want to secure a decent place.

So, how are this church and this story related to the second church the "Madonna Della Salute"? Simple, while people were still giving thanks to the Lord for dispensing them of the plague there was a new outbreak about 50 years later, in 1630. This second outbreak was even more violent and people were dying faster than before. So the city ruler had to act quickly and do something. Building some more hospitals in which to keep the sick far from the healthy was out of any question so he came up with a new bright idea: promise to build a church and to have people going to adore the Virgin Mary once a year but only if the Virgin first stopped the plague. The idea must have pleased her since suddenly the plague outbreak receded! About 50000 had died in a few months, more than in the previous outbreak that lasted 2 years but what mattered most was that it stopped. So they went on, built the "Madonna Della Salute" church and declared that every year, on the 4th of November a procession was to be held and all citizens should go and adore the Virgin. This continues to the present day. On the 4th of November, a floating bridge is built between S.Marco square and the church so that pilgrims can reach the church without flooding the narrow alleys we will later walk when we will come quite close to this church.

At the time of writing Google satellite view shows this bridge. So you can now go and propose a riddle to your friends: can you tell on which day of the year the aerial picture was shot? Of course, the date is the 4th of November since it's the only day of the year when a floating bridge is built between "S.Marco" and the "Madonna Della Salute" church.

Venice off the Beaten Track

N.Cimmino

Women that count

Let's head back to the square and, about halfway on the northside of it, turn into "Calle Dei Fabbri" ("Blacksmiths Alley"), under the porch. If we keep walking straight, after a few bridges and an alley name change we come to water. This is where common sense suggests to stop walking and either take a turn or start to swim. We will turn left into "Riva del Carbon" ("Charcoal Waterfront"). This place is so-called because it used to be where boats bringing charcoal into town would unload and where charcoal storages were located. On the other side of the water is "Riva del Vin" ("Wine Waterfront") but I have no idea why this name was given, someone brighter than me might have a guess. On the right side is the Rialto bridge, one of the most iconic pieces of Venice and, exactly for this reason, we will leave it for much later after more interesting things. If we walk a bit along the waterfront we come to Ca'Farsetti, which nowadays is the town hall. A plaque on the corner reminds us that in this house Elena Cornaro Piscopia was born, sometimes in 1646. About 50% of people born in Venice were female and, to honour the truth, women were not kept in such a high consideration at the time. So what makes this specific person worth a plaque? She was, after going through a lot of trouble, the first woman in the world to get a university degree. If you think your university teacher has been unfair to you, hear what happened to this poor girl. She always showed an interest in maths since childhood but, as it was the case at the time, she stood no chance to study something that was regarded as a chiefly male pursuit. After some difficulties she managed to get into the Theology faculty in Padova and, even though the subject was not as scientifically accurate at maths, things seemed to be going well. But not for long, when the bishop found out that a woman dared to undertake theology studies he forbade the university to allow her to pursue the degree and, clearly, the university, being the lay institution we know it was, obeyed immediately and radiated her. She managed eventually to get a degree in philosophy and, what matters most, to be the first woman with a university degree.

Magic Potions

Let's head back through "Calle del Carbon", right into "Campo Manin" and more or less straight till we come to "Campo S.Stefano". Why is this place called "Campo S.Stefano"? Easy: there is a church called S.Stefano in this square. But the reason we are here is not the church but a rather inconspicuous floor tile that is at the corner with "Calle Spezier" ("Chemist Alley"). Here we will admire one of the tiles on the ground that has a circular depression in it. What caused this? There is a long story behind, a story that goes back to the 1600s. At that time a potion was invented, apparently in Venice, that went under the name of "Teriaca". This was a potion that could cure pretty much any ailment known at the time so, as you might expect, it was very popular and expensive. As things go when something is in high demand and expensive someone sooner or later gets the idea to forge it and make even more profit. To prevent fraud, "Teriaca" production was strictly regulated. Only a handful of chemists had a licence to produce it in Venice and they were subject to strict rules. Every time a new batch was prepared the ingredients, among which were vipers, had to be exposed for three days in front of the chemist shop so that people could go by and verify the genuineness of the products. The system was not foolproof since one of the ingredients the recipe called for was "unicorn powder" which, as you could expect, was a bit hard to come by. Apparently, a narwhal tusk was used and people didn't know better which is understandable since they didn't have the internet back then.

A mark impressed in the pavement stones, formed under the weight and heat of the cauldrons used to prepare "Teriaca". (Photo N.Cimmino 2015)

Once the three days had passed, with a magistrate called as a witness, the preparation would start. Teriaca was cooked in huge cauldrons in front of the chemist shops. And it's one of the three legs of one of these heavy cauldrons that, in time, left the mark we are here to admire. If you feel like treasure hunting you can go and find the other two. They are scattered somewhere around the court as paving stones have been moved around during maintenance works in the centuries.

On a more contemporary note, in this corner we can also find a rather interesting modern art shop, you will recognize it from a flashing green cross sign of the type usually used by chemist shops. Aside from the modern art inside, which might be of interest to some, is the sign on the door that, in Italian, reads "I might be open sometimes, when I feel like it", a sure guarantee that the artist himself is running the shop.

Let's move south and cross the Grand Canal on Accademia bridge (it's either that or swimming, you choose). The "Accademia" bridge is an interesting one. Made in wood, it was built at the beginning of the 1900s. There are rumours of plans to replace it with an ugly metal structure, fortunately, it seems the project won't go ahead.

If we keep moving south we come, once more, to water. If you have been particularly impressed by the "Madonna Della Salute" church you can here turn left and go all the way down to it, perhaps a 15 min detour. It's a nice place to be so it might be worth the extra time. We will continue here on the right, which is towards the west, along Fondamenta Zattere.

Sunset over the lagoon from Fondamenta Zattere.

(Photo N.Cimmino 2017)

Zattere and Squero

A famous ice-cream parlour on this riverside is "Gelateria Nico". If you decide to stop here for an ice treat consider ordering their "Gianduiotto", they are renowned for it and you will not be disappointed (please remind me to claim my 10% discount I just awarded myself for mentioning this). Once done stuffing ourselves in ice-cream let's move on towards west and turn right into "Rio S.Trovaso". This is one of the little corners of Venice I particularly like. It's not much different than other places but the narrow canal, with waterside on both sides and the overall atmosphere, have a particular appeal. You might simply dislike it, sorry about that, your problem. There is however a very important reason for us to be here. Along this canal, we can see one of the few "Squero" left in Venice.

The "Squero" is a place where gondolas are built and repaired. Apparently, the name comes from "Squadra", a set square which is a rather unusual instrument, if you ask me, to be used in building something that must have close to no right angles. Gondolas have a long history in Venice and have been the most common means of transport before motorized boats came along.

The shape of gondolas changed in time and has been refined to make them more stable and easier to steer. A gondola consists of 260 different parts, made with 6 different types of wood. It's 11 meters long and is propelled using a single paddle. For this reason, being the thrust asymmetric, the oarsman stands on one side.

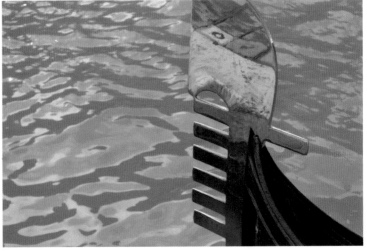

The author assumed for many years this was just an ornament
with no particular meaning, he did some research and what he found
will shock you.
(Photo M.Fleischer 2015)

Shifting his weight from one side to another he causes the inclination of the vessel to change which, in turn, assists with steering.

The gondola's bow has a characteristic metallic decoration that, before I started researching the subject, I thought was just something randomly designed to look nice. It turns out it represents pretty much anything in Venice from the 6 districts to the major islands (Murano, Burano, Torcello), the Grand Canal, Rialto Bridge and even the typical hat worn by the city ruler back in the times. To be honest, you need a lot of fantasy to see all this but, who am I to disprove such a claim?

Let's now cross the canal, possibly on a bridge, and head west into Calle Toletta. We will pass "Bar Alla Toletta", one of my favourites for a Cappuccino and some sweet pastry. Let's move on and pass Libreria Toletta a huge (in fact several shops on both sides of the alley) bookshop with a lot of interesting books, including some in English. We finally turn right into Calle Cerchieri and follow it to Palazzo Loredan.

View on a "Squero", where gondolas are made.

(Photo M.Fleischer 2015)

Palazzo Loredan

This palace belonged to Vettor Calergi sometimes in the 1600s. Being the nice guy he was, he decided, at his death, to leave it as an inheritance to his sister's sons. It's unclear to me why not to the sister but it might be related to the high consideration women were kept into back in those days. These sons of a sister though were not so nice guys. One day they kidnapped a guy that, for reasons unknown to us, was their rival, a certain Francesco Querini. This one is not to be confused with the Italian explorer by the same name, who lost his life in a polar expedition in 1900. Incidentally, all he got in exchange for his life was a lousy island named after him. The Querini of this story was much more fortunate as he didn't need to go all the way to the north pole to meet his fate. The aforementioned sons of a sister took him to their palace and, after torturing him, they had an exotic animal, namely a tiger, devour him. He died after being eaten alive, which was an unexpected side effect for the sons of a sister. Someone thought this was not very kind of them, so they have been expelled from Venice. You might remember the baker that was sentenced to death for a crime he didn't commit just one century before. Apparently, judges became much more tolerant and just expelled convicted murderers. But the judges did more: they ordered the wing of the palace where the murder took place to be destroyed and a column of shame to be erected in its place. Surprisingly, or not so surprising perhaps, these nice sons of a sister were admitted back to Venice just a few years later when they offered a great sum of money to support the war Venice was waging against the Turkish.

Casin Dei Nobili

Let's head back to Fondamenta Toletta and proceed north, just a few hundred meters till we reach a passage under a house named "Sottoportego Casin Dei Nobili". What is "Casin"? It means "Little House", so this would be the porch of the nobleman's little house which, to be honest, doesn't sound anything interesting. The word "casino" in truth indicated a place, sometimes just a room, that certain groups of persons used to meet secretly and abandon themselves to every kind of mundane activity, primarily gambling.

Venice has a long history related to gambling. It all started back in the 1100s. Someone brought back as war trophy three large and heavy columns of granite. One was lost at sea while unloading it in Piazza S.Marco, the other two were laid on the pavement by the side of S.Marco church as nobody knew how, or wanted to take responsibility, to erect them. The obvious solution would have been to show them a female column, but they didn't come with that idea. So the city ruler eventually started to look for people ready to take the risk to lift the heavy and fragile war trophy. Many refused, probably afraid to be beheaded should the precious mementoes end up in smithereens. Things changed when Niccolò Barattieri came along. An expert builder he, or supposedly his employees, lifted the two columns exactly where we see them nowadays in Piazzetta S.Marco (not to be confused with Piazza, this is the little one on the side of S.Marco Church). Anyhow, back to gambling. The guy eventually managed to safely raise the columns as we see them still nowadays. The city ruler was particularly pleased that they were standing and still in one piece so offered the guy to express any wish. The guy asked to authorize gambling, which was forbidden, on the little square where the columns were erected. The ruler agreed and the first gambling square of the world was born. Since then gambling became very popular, especially among noblemen that could afford to lose large sums. They were also allowed to wear masks for a good part of the year so they were playing even in broad daylight in the cafes without being recognizable. But, mainly, they used to play at night in these private places where unmasked they could take the occasion to socialize with other influential personalities and play not only cards but their power games too. Under the porch, near the door, we can see a small square hole, that was a peephole used to check who knocked at the door before opening.

Let's once more walk north till we reach water and turn left in Fondamenta Gherardini. The first bridge on the left is the one we are looking for.

A view of "Ponte Dei Pugni". If you want to feel like a local and do your health a favour in the process, go ahead and get yourself some fruit too. I bet the fruit aisle in your department store back home doesn't look quite the same.

(Photo N.Cimmino 2015)

A quiet canal reflects the palaces on its surface.

(Photo N.Cimmino 2018)

Ponte Dei Pugni

This is a quite unremarkable bridge in appearance. It's a nice spot where a barge several days a week stops and sells vegetables and fruit directly to people on the waterfront. But that's not the reason we have come all the way here. We are here for the bridge. Its name means "punches bridge". Why in Venice would a bridge have such a violent name? That's because this very bridge used to be where fierce fights between two opposing gangs in Venice took place.

Fights started back in the 1300s between Castellani and Nicolotti. Castellani lived in Castello, the eastmost district of Venice and mainly worked at the arsenal building ships. Nicolotti, the name from S.Nicolo' church, lived in the west and were mainly fishermen. For reasons unknown to us, and most likely to them as well, they hated each other for centuries and were regularly challenging each other in tournaments that were taking place between September and Christmas (please don't ask, I don't know what they did the rest of the year). The tournaments had strict rules and were of many different types. In some instances, it was a one to one fight, in others many against many. The guys fought on the bridge and often ended up falling into the canal. There was a lot of blood being shed and many were injured, but only seldom someone died. Things kept going till the 1700s when the fights have been ruled as illegal. Since then the two gangs faced each other during Carnival in so-called "Forze d'Ercole" which, compared to the previous brutal fights were really kindergarten games. In these games, members of the two gangs had to form as a human pyramid as high as possible by standing on each other's shoulders. The gang forming the highest pyramid won. I presume midgets and dwarves were excluded from the game.

As far as I know, this tradition is not anymore alive and people entertain themselves in different ways for carnival such as getting drunk in the alleys or indulging in legal highs.

Let's move on to Campo Santa Margherita, San Pantalon and Basilica dei Frari, Campo S.Stin, Calle della Vida, Calle Chiesa, Calle seconda del Cristo, Calle Agnello all the way to Ponte delle Tette.

Not much to see here along the way, or I just haven't been diligent enough in my research. So, this was a bit of a long walk, get out your google maps if you got lost and make sure you are at "Ponte Delle Tette".

Ponte Delle Tette

So, previously, we have been through Ponte Tetta. Which sounded almost like "female breast" but, boringly enough for the boys, turned out to be just someone's surname. This, though, is the real stuff. This bridge is named after the female body part.

Why would someone give such a name to a bridge? Well, a first hint is that we are in an area of Venice known as "Carampane" which was, fundamentally the redlight district of the city. It seems sometimes in the 1700s the city ruler started to be concerned about "men sinning against nature" which really, was just a discriminatory and long way to say homosexuals or gay which has the benefit of being even shorter. Being the good ruler and smart person he thought he was, he decided to offer a free cure for this awful disease that was devouring his city: he instructed all prostitutes to wear no clothing when they were enticing their customers from the windows of the palace. It's not clear what the conversion rate was but, to be honest, I think it was close to zero. Nonetheless, people started to call this bridge "Tits Bridge", owing to the views that could be admired while walking on it. The name, like all the others, stuck in time even after a wave of puritanism that culminated in a 1958 law that forced to close all brothels in Italy.

Let's continue south-east towards "S.Silvestro" till we come to the Grand Canal again, this time on the other side. Riva del Vin (wine waterfront). As mentioned before, when we were in Riva del Carbon (charcoal waterfront) this side is so-called because boats bringing wine to the city used to unload here the wine and wine warehouses were along this waterfront. It's unclear why the other side is called "charcoal waterfront" but maybe someone more clever than me can figure it out.

Barbacane

Let's walk north along Riva del Vin till we find "Calle Della Madonna" on the left. Few tens of meters inside the alley we are greeted by this wonderful piece of history that many overlooked. In fact, I know of locals that have no idea what this is about. This is a "Barbacane" a word that shares some roots with "barbican", which is the external fortification of a castle. In this case, the word was used in Venetian architecture to indicate an extension to the higher floors of the houses that allowed to get extra space without reducing the space available in the alley. It was also welcomed by people as it provided some protection from the rain. Some guys though started to overdo it and alleys often were left with not enough light or ventilation which made them very unhealthy. So the city ruler decided to put a limit to the size of the extension and placed here a reference "Barbacane" that served as a model of the maximum allowed size. Moving along the alley we can see this architectural solution used in the houses on both sides.

A reference "Barbacane". This is one of many that were installed
around the city to sanction the maximum allowed
size for such artefacts.
(Photo N.Cimmino 2017)

At the end of the alley, we turn right into Ruga
Vecchia S. Giovanni and eventually come to Rialto
fish market.

Fish and talking statues

There is a lot to say in this little square in front of S.Giacometto church. First of all let's recall we are now in Rialto, which was the first settlement in Venice. The church of S.Giacometto is said to be the first church in Venice. It has been rebuilt since the first instalment dates back to the 400CE. The actual building should be from the 1100s with some preservation and renovation work done through the centuries.

This was the area where most markets were and, along with with the markets the warehouses and the first banks. Nowadays a very active and well-stocked fish market takes place every morning except on Sundays as the fragrance of the area testifies.

If you turn around, keeping your back to the church, you will notice the statue of a man carrying quite a massive stone over his shoulders. This is known as the "Hunchback of Rialto" but, to be honest, I don't think he was even hunchback, it's just that they gave him such a burden he couldn't possibly stand.

What is this statue anyway? The thing is a podium on which a guy used to stand and announce sentences for the convicted criminals. Those responsible for minor felonies were stripped naked and made run along the streets from S.Marco to here while people on the side of the road threw stuff at them while shouting insults. Once they reached the hunchback their names and crimes were announced by the guy standing on the podium and the felon was given a chance to kiss the statue to save himself from further humiliation.

The hunchback holding the weight of the crime and, truth be told, of a bit of stone too.
(Photo N.Cimmino 2017)

Punishments were not always that mild though, for severe crimes death was the penalty. A long agony awaited the convict, who was often towed by a horse on the street, tortured, mutilated and eventually left to die. More details on this in another story we will come to later.

There is something else interesting about this podium or statue. It seems it's part of a group of statues that talk. It was in the 1700s that a statue in Rome, Pasquino, started to speak. The drunkest ones heard sounds from his mouth, the sober though noticed from time to time, in the early mornings, notes affixed to the pedestal of the statue. Notes that were often accusations against the Pope and the church in general. The thing is, at some point, this started to happen also to this statue in Rialto where poems and rhymes accusing the government or some cardinals appeared, in the same fashion as in Rome: always in the early mornings. It was, clearly, a very important way for people to express "freely" in a society that surely didn't allow much in terms of expressing one's opinion.

You can have a look at Rialto bridge, that's what all tourists do, so you probably did already. We can then move west along Calle Miani, Campo S.Cassiano, S.Giacomo dall'Orio and eventually north Riva de Biasio. I am not claiming there is nothing to see along the way, just I haven't found anything interesting to tell.

There is however one little curiosity we can have a look at if you want to take a couple of extra steps. As we pass the fish market, cross it walking towards the Grand Canal. On the north wall is an old plaque that reports the minimum size of fishes, by species, that can be legally sold. This was an attempt to prevent resources depletion in the lagoon, giving time to the fish to reproduce before they were put on sale. As seen in the picture, not sure has it been wiped clean by now, someone thought it was a good idea to make an addition to the bottom of the plaque with a black marker. To understand what's going on you will need to know that, in Venetian dialect, fish is also slang for penis. So someone felt appropriate to add "mine" followed by what looks anyway a ridiculously small size to be proud of, just 28.5 cm, I know, I know stupid kids.

De Biasio

So why are we in Riva de Biasio? This waterfront gives the name to a waterbus stop, and it's a very remarkable stop. It is the only waterbus stop on the Grand Canal that is not named after a famous Palace or a saint but after an everyday man: "Biagio Cargnio". To be honest, he, fortunately, was not your everyday man though he looked so to the hundreds of customers that every day visited his shop, a butchery, that was known all over Venice and outside for the most delicious sausages humankind ever tasted. Surely they must have been good if a waterfront and water bus stop still has his name after centuries! But it's not for the taste of his sausages that Mr Biagio is remembered to the present day. Let's see what happened on an otherwise uneventful day many centuries ago. A guy, who bought some sausages at Biagio's shop had them cooked by his wife. He was sitting and savouring his delicious meal when he found something chunkier than usual. Upon inspection it turned out to be a thumb, a rather small one, perhaps belonging to a child! So he ran to find the police who had Biagio arrested while they searched his shop. The bodies of several children, in different stages of dismemberment, were found. At that point, Biagio confessed that his secret ingredient for the sausages was indeed children's flesh.

He was eventually declared guilty and, as anticipated when we were in Rialto, he was not given a little pat on the back for his misbehaviour. He got tied to a horse and has been towed around the city streets. Once in "S.Marco", his hands were chopped off and he was tortured and left to die slowly. They also destroyed his shop but people kept calling the waterfront by his name. Alright, enough talking, it's time for dinner! There is a very nice restaurant behind the corner, they serve the best sausages in town...wait, where did I hear this already?

Let's instead walk to S.Simeone Profeta, Calle Lunga and again by the waterfront and stop at S.Simeone Piccolo church.

Small things

S.Simeone Piccolo means "Little St.Simon" which I don't think refers to the stature of Simon, but to the fact that this church is smaller than the other S.Simeone church we just passed. Short was the stature of a french guy that, sometimes at the end of the 1700s, came to Venice to invade it. Once he saw this church he asserted: "I have seen churches with no domes, but never domes without a church", clearly referring to the rather peculiar shape of this church.

We are not done with small things yet. Let's move southwest towards "Fondamenta Dei Tolentini". Here we find a bookshop "Un mare di carta" that sells a lot of nautical literature. I know you won't care but here I got a very nice book about weather. They also sell little models of boats and gondolas made of cardboard or plywood to assemble. If you are inclined to pursue such a hobby this could be a good spot where to look for what you need.

Continuing south we come to another little thing. "Bacareto da Lele". What is "Bacaretto"? It's a small "Bacaro". What is "Bacaro"? It's a place where you can get "Cicheti"! Yes, I know you don't know what they are. Cicheti are small (see, small, as in the chapter theme) food portions used as starters and washed down usually with an aperitif. This is where I would like to end our walk with some fried octopus, polenta and spritz (the aperitif). I hope you enjoyed this little tour and the anecdotes I shared. I will leave you to your food and drinks.

Ciao!

(A word originating from the Venetian "Sciavo", contraction of "Sciavo Vostro" meaning "I am your slave". Now don't get funny ideas, no kinky business. It's just the way we greet people over here....or is it?....oh my....)

If you feel like getting lost in some good reading, after getting lost in Venice, I suggest you grab a copy of Leon Kaminsky "Celluloid Ham" book and learn more about little-known stories[8] from the world of cinema while you sip your aperitif.

https://www.amazon.co.uk/dp/B0821SP8RK

---

[8] Real ones, not like mine where Michael Radford inspired Shakespeare which, I hope, came through as a joke.

One of many colourful, and usually bitter, aperitives available.
(Photo N.Cimmino 2019)

Printed in Germany
by Amazon Distribution
GmbH, Leipzig

18658903R00059